Collins

Reading

KS2 English Reading

D0524943

SATs Question Book

Age 10 – 11

Key Stage 2

SATs Question Book

Alison Head

Contents

- You will need to use the pull-out reading booklet in the centre of this book to answer the questions.

- There are different types of question for you to answer in different ways. The space for your answer shows you what type of answer is needed.

- Some questions are multiple choice, some are short answers where you need only write a word or a few words, and others are longer and followed by several lines to give you space to write more words or a sentence or two.

- Always read the instructions carefully so that you know how to answer each question.

- The number of marks for each question will help you to know how much detail you need to give in your answer.

- There are three progress tests throughout the book to allow you to practise the skills again. Record your results in the progress charts to identify what you are doing well in and what you can improve.

Acknowledgements

Images © Shutterstock.com
Every effort has been made to trace copyright holders and obtain their permission for the use of copyright material. The author and publisher will gladly receive information enabling them to rectify any error or omission in subsequent editions. All facts are correct at time of going to press.

Published by Collins
An imprint of HarperCollins*Publishers*
1 London Bridge Street,
London SE1 9GF

© HarperCollins*Publishers* Limited

ISBN 9780008201593

First published 2016

10 9 8 7 6 5 4 3 2 1

All rights reserved. No part of this publication may be reproduced, stored in a retrieval system, or transmitted, in any form or by any means, electronic, mechanical, photocopying, recording or otherwise, without the prior permission of Collins.

British Library Cataloguing in Publication Data.

A CIP record of this book is available from the British Library.

Commissioning Editor: Michelle I'Anson
Author: Alison Head
Project Management and Editorial: Fiona Kyle and Katie Galloway
Cover Design: Sarah Duxbury and Paul Oates
Inside Concept Design: Paul Oates and Ian Wrigley
Text Design and Layout: Contentra Technologies
Production: Lyndsey Rogers
Printed and bound in China by RR Donnelley APS

Choosing the Meaning of Words in Context

> These questions are about *The Secret Garden*.

1 *every morning she ate her breakfast in the nursery which had nothing amusing in it...*

In this sentence, the word *amusing* is closest in meaning to...

comical ☐

amazing ☐

interesting ☑

modern ☐

1 mark

2 *she gazed out of the window across to the huge moor...*

In this sentence, the word *gazed* is closest in meaning to...

glared ☐

stared ☑

climbed ☐

glanced ☐

1 mark

3 *when she began to walk quickly or even run along the paths and down the avenue, she was stirring her slow blood...*

In this sentence, the word *stirring* is closest in meaning to...

mixing ✓

resting ☐

moving ☐

rushing ☐

1 mark

4 *wandered about the paths in the park...*

In this sentence, the word *wandered* is closest in meaning to...

hurried ☐

crept ✓

sauntered ☐

pondered ☐

1 mark

Total marks .... /4

How am I doing?

Giving the Meaning of Words in Context

These questions are about *The Secret Garden.*

1 In the first paragraph, **find** and **copy** one word that suggests that the wind is noisy.

The blazing is sure lad.

1 mark

2 In the paragraph that begins *One place she went to oftener than to any other...* **find** and **copy** a word that tells you that there is nothing growing in the flower beds.

1 mark

3 In the paragraph that begins *A few days after...* **find** and **copy** two words that tell you about the colour of the bird.

2 marks

4 In the paragraph that begins *I like you!*, **find** and **copy** a word that describes how fast the robin flies to the tree.

1 mark

5 Circle the correct word to complete the sentence below.

At the end of the second paragraph Mary Lennox did not look at her porridge…

| despairingly | scornfully | hungrily | rudely |

1 mark

6 Circle the correct word to complete the sentence below.

When he does not talk to her, Mary thinks that Ben Weatherstaff is too busy or too…

| flustered | shy | rude | angry |

1 mark

7 Circle the correct word to complete the sentence below.

Mary notices that one part of the wall has been…

| ruined | shunned | forgotten | damaged |

1 mark

8 Circle the correct word to complete the sentence below.

Before she meets the robin, Mary's appearance is described as thin, ugly and…

| shallow | grey | pale | tall |

1 mark

Total marks …………. /9   How am I doing?

Explaining the Meaning of Words in Context

> **Questions 1–3 are about *The Way Through the Woods.***

1 In the third line of the poem, explain what the word *undone* suggests about what has happened to the road.

_____

_____

_____

1 mark

2 *the badgers roll at ease…*

Explain what the words *at ease* suggest about the badgers.

_____

_____

_____

1 mark

3 *You will hear the beat of a horse's feet…*

Explain what the word *beat* suggests about the sound the poet is describing.

_____

_____

_____

1 mark

Explaining the Meaning of Words in Context

4 Explain **two** things that the words *kind big smile* suggest about what the poet thinks about the sky.

_____

_____

_____ 2 marks

5 Explain what the word *lace* suggests about the leaves on the tree.

_____

_____

_____ 1 mark

6 Explain what the word *kisses* suggests about how the sun feels on the poet's face.

_____

_____

_____ 1 mark

Total marks .... /7   How am I doing?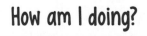

9

Finding Meaning from Words

Questions 1–3 are about *The Olympic Games.*

1 *Historic manuscripts* (page 7)

What does this tell you about the information we have about the ancient Olympic Games?

_____

_____ 1 mark

2 *revived by Frenchman Baron Pierre de Coubertin* (page 7)

What does this tell you about Baron Pierre de Coubertin's role in the modern Olympic Games?

_____

_____ 1 mark

3 *fierce competition*

What does this tell you about London's bid to host the 2012 Olympic Games?

_____

_____ 1 mark

Questions 4–6 are about *Moonfleet*.

---

4 *my heart fell to thumping* (page 9)

What does this tell you about the strength of the narrator's emotions?

_____

_____ 1 mark

5 *wriggling my body up under the tombstone* (page 10)

What does this tell you about how much space there was in the opening of the passage?

_____

_____ 1 mark

6 Look at the first paragraph: *the crack in the ground had still further widened, just where it came up to the tomb…*

Find and **copy** four other words in this paragraph that mean an opening in the ground.

1. _____

2. _____

3. _____

4. _____ 4 marks

| Total marks .... /9 | How am I doing? |

Progress Test I

These questions are about *Moonfleet*.

1 *I perceived that there was under the monument a larger cavity...*

In this sentence, the word *perceived* is closest in meaning to...

understood ☐

guessed ☐

sensed ☐

observed ☐

1 mark

2 *perhaps even to Blackbeard's hoard...*

In this sentence, the word *hoard* is closest in meaning to...

store ☐

clue ☐

crowd ☐

crew ☐

1 mark

3 In the first paragraph, **find** and **copy** one word that tells you that the crack in the ground has got bigger.

_____

1 mark

4 *I had constantly before my eyes a vision*

What does this tell you about how often the narrator thought about the story of Bluebeard's diamond?

_____

_____

1 mark

5 Circle the correct word to complete the sentence below.

The narrator was surprised that the passage did not seem to be...

| abandoned | empty | damp | dark |

1 mark

6 Explain what the word *trodden* suggests about the passage.

_____

_____

1 mark

Total marks .... /6   How am I doing?

13

These questions are about *The Secret Garden.*

1 What does Mary Lennox do every morning?

Give **two** things.

1. _____

   _____

2. _____

   _____

2 marks

2 What does Mary eat for *each breakfast*?

_____

1 mark

3 *big breaths of rough fresh air*?

Which of Mary's features is *brightened* by the fresh air. Circle on the picture blow.

1 mark

4 How many people live in Martha's cottage?

_____

1 mark

5 Circle the correct word to complete each sentence below.

a) Every morning, Mary awakes to Martha kneeling at the...

| tapestry | fireplace | floor | window ledge |

1 mark

b) When Mary walks towards Ben Weatherstaff he turns away...

| immediately | deliberately | accidentally | suddenly |

1 mark

c) The ivy on part of the wall had not been...

| green | clipped | creeping | bare |

1 mark

d) The robin makes a brilliant...

| gleam | flash | chirp | colour |

1 mark

Total marks .... /9   How am I doing? 😊 😐 😣

Finding Information in Fiction 2

These questions are about *Moonfleet.*

1 At what time of day does this part of the story take place?

_____

_____ 1 mark

2 Who told the boy the story of Blackbeard's treasure?

_____ 1 mark

3 a) How broad was the passage?

_____ 1 mark

b) How high was the passage?

_____ 1 mark

4 What has the passage been cut through?

_____ 1 mark

5 What has made the *trail* on the floor of the passage?

_____

_____   1 mark

6 Circle the correct word to complete each sentence below.

a) A hole appears at the tomb's...

| floor | edge | grass | grave |

1 mark

b) The boy slipped into the hole...

| head-first | feet-first | reluctantly | nervously |

1 mark

c) The passage was cut through...

| earth | grass | brick | stone |

1 mark

d) The boy left the passage because he was afraid of the...

| churchyard | pitfalls | darkness | tomb |

1 mark

Total marks .... /10   How am I doing?

Finding Information in Poetry

1 How many years ago was the road through the woods closed?

_____

1 mark

2 How do the animals in the wood behave where the road used to be?

Give **two** ways.

1. _____

2. _____

2 marks

3 Circle the correct word to complete the sentence.

The otter signals to its mate with a…

| swish | splash | whistle | whisper |

1 mark

4 Circle the correct word to complete the sentence.

The rings in the water of the pool are made by…

| ring-doves | trout | otters | horses |

1 mark

Questions 5–8 are about *Friends.*

5 What is the child in the poem looking up through?

_____

1 mark

6 The child writes that three natural things are like friends. Apart from the Sunshine, what are the other **two**?

1. _____

2. _____

2 marks

7 *The Sunshine flickers through the lace*

What part of the tree do these words describe?

Circle the part of the tree in the picture.

1 mark

8 Which family member is mentioned in the poem?

_____

1 mark

Total marks .... /10   How am I doing?

Finding Information in Non-Fiction 1

These questions are about *The Olympic Games*.

1 Look at the section *The First Olympic Games.*

Complete the table.

When did the first Olympic Games take place?	
To which god were they dedicated?	
How often did the games take place?	

2 marks

According to the text, what were the main sports at the first Olympic Games?

Give **two** examples:

1. _____

2. _____

2 marks

What did Baron Pierre de Coubertin believe sport could do?

_____

_____

1 mark

4 The London 2012 Olympic Park was the size of how many football pitches?

_____ 1 mark

5 Match the events to the year in which they happened.

The Ancient Olympics were abolished	330 BC
The Panathenaic Stadium was built	393 AD
The Olympic symbol was designed	1976
The first Paralympic Winter Games were held	1913

1 mark

6 Why was the 1908 Olympic Games moved from Italy to the United Kingdom?

_____

_____

_____

_____ 1 mark

Total marks .... /8   How am I doing?

21

Finding Information in Non-Fiction 2

> ## These questions are about *Love your heart!*

1 What makes sure the blood in your heart flows in the right direction?

_____

1 mark

2 Tick **true** or **false** in the table for each piece of information about the human heart.

	True	False
Human hearts have two chambers.		
Arteries carry blood away from the heart.		
Your pulse rate is how many times your heart beats in a minute.		
Your heart is around the same size as your head.		

1 mark

3 What happens to your pulse rate when you exercise?

_____

1 mark

4 What does your blood collect from the air you breathe and carry to your muscles?

_____

1 mark

5 How many times does the average heart beat each day?

_____ 1 mark

6 Look at page 12.

According to the text, what should you eat to help keep your heart healthy?

Give **two** things.

1. _____

2. _____ 2 marks

7 What happens to your heart and lungs if you make them work harder?

_____ 1 mark

| Total marks ..../8 | How am I doing? |

Summarising Main Ideas

Question 1 is about *The Way Through the Woods.*

1 What is the main message of the poem *The Way Through the Woods?*

Tick **one.**

You can no longer drive through the woods. ☐

Animals that live in the woods are not afraid of people. ☐

Nature reclaims land when humans abandon it. ☐

It takes 70 years for a forest to grow. ☐

1 mark

Question 2 is about *Friends.*

2 What is the main message of the poem *Friends?*

Tick **one.**

Sunny days make you feel happy. ☐

You should never feel lonely when you are surrounded by nature. ☐

Under a tree is a good place to rest if you are tired. ☐

The wind is invisible. ☐

1 mark

Question 3 is about *The Secret Garden*.

3 Using information from the text, *The Secret Garden*, tick a box in each row to say whether each statement is **true** or **false**.

	True	False
Mary spends time in the garden because there is nothing to do indoors.		
Mary does not like Ben Weatherstaff.		
Martha thinks that being outside is good for Mary's health.		
Mary is not curious about the walled garden.		

1 mark

Question 4 is about *Moonfleet*.

4 Using information from the text, *Moonfleet,* tick a box in each row to say whether each statement is **true** or **false**.

	True	False
The events in the extract take place in a churchyard.		
The boy is not interested in what is under the grave.		
The passage is man-made.		
The boy is the first person to have walked along the passage.		

1 mark

Total marks .... /4   How am I doing?

Progress Test 2

1 How does the boy know that it is after four o'clock in the afternoon?

_____

_____ 1 mark

2 The boy takes care when he explores the underground passage.

Give **two** ways in which he does this.

1. _____

_____

2. _____

_____ 2 marks

Questions 3–5 are about *The Way Through the Woods*.

3 What is the road *underneath*?

Give **two** things.

1. _____

2. _____ 2 marks

The Secret Garden

The Way Through the Woods

Friends

The Olympic Games

Moonfleet

Love Your Heart!

Reading booklet

Key Stage 2 English reading booklet

Contents

The Secret Garden

At first each day which passed by for Mary Lennox was exactly like the others. Every morning she awoke in her tapestried room and found Martha kneeling upon the hearth building her fire; every morning she ate her breakfast in the nursery which had nothing amusing in it; and after each breakfast she gazed out of the window across to the huge moor which seemed to spread out on all sides and climb up to the sky, and after she had stared for a while she realised that if she did not go out she would have to stay in and do nothing—and so she went out. She did not know that this was the best thing she could have done, and she did not know that, when she began to walk quickly or even run along the paths and down the avenue, she was stirring her slow blood and making herself stronger by fighting with the wind which swept down from the moor. She ran only to make herself warm, and she hated the wind which rushed at her face and roared and held her back as if it were some giant she could not see. But the big breaths of rough fresh air blown over the heather filled her lungs with something which was good for her whole thin body and whipped some red colour into her cheeks and brightened her dull eyes when she did not know anything about it.

But after a few days spent almost entirely out of doors she wakened one morning knowing what it was to be hungry, and when she sat down to her breakfast she did not glance disdainfully at her porridge and push it away, but took up her spoon and began to eat it and went on eating it until her bowl was empty.

"Tha' got on well enough with that this mornin', didn't tha'?" said Martha.

"It tastes nice today," said Mary, feeling a little surprised herself.

"It's th' air of th' moor that's givin' thee stomach for tha' victuals," answered Martha. "It's lucky for thee that tha's got victuals as well as appetite. There's been twelve in our cottage as had th' stomach an' nothin' to put in it. You go on playin' you out o' doors every day an' you'll get some flesh on your bones an' you won't be so yeller."

"I don't play," said Mary. "I have nothing to play with."

"Nothin' to play with!" exclaimed Martha. "Our children plays with sticks and stones. They just runs about an' shouts an' looks at things." Mary did not shout, but she looked at things. There was nothing else to do. She walked round and round the gardens and wandered about the paths in the park. Sometimes she looked for Ben

Weatherstaff, but though several times she saw him at work he was too busy to look at her or was too surly. Once when she was walking toward him he picked up his spade and turned away as if he did it on purpose.

One place she went to oftener than to any other. It was the long walk outside the gardens with the walls round them. There were bare flower-beds on either side of it and against the walls ivy grew thickly. There was one part of the wall where the creeping dark green leaves were more bushy than elsewhere. It seemed as if for a long time that part had been neglected. The rest of it had been clipped and made to look neat, but at this lower end of the walk it had not been trimmed at all.

A few days after she had talked to Ben Weatherstaff, Mary stopped to notice this and wondered why it was so. She had just paused and was looking up at a long spray of ivy swinging in the wind when she saw a gleam of scarlet and heard a brilliant chirp, and there, on the top of the wall, forward perched Ben Weatherstaff's robin redbreast, tilting forward to look at her with his small head on one side.

"Oh!" she cried out, "is it you—is it you?" And it did not seem at all queer to her that she spoke to him as if she were sure that he would understand and answer her.

He did answer. He twittered and chirped and hopped along the wall as if he were telling her all sorts of things. It seemed to Mistress Mary as if she understood him, too, though he was not speaking in words. It was as if he said:

"Good morning! Isn't the wind nice? Isn't the sun nice? Isn't everything nice? Let us both chirp and hop and twitter. Come on! Come on!"

Mary began to laugh, and as he hopped and took little flights along the wall she ran after him. Poor little thin, sallow, ugly Mary—she actually looked almost pretty for a moment.

"I like you! I like you!" she cried out, pattering down the walk; and she chirped and tried to whistle, which last she did not know how to do in the least. But the robin seemed to be quite satisfied and chirped and whistled back at her. At last he spread his wings and made a darting flight to the top of a tree, where he perched and sang loudly. That reminded Mary of the first time she had seen him. He had been swinging on a tree-top then and she had been standing in the orchard. Now she was on the other side of the orchard and standing in the path outside a wall—much lower down—and there was the same tree inside.

"It's in the garden no one can go into," she said to herself. "It's the garden without a door. He lives in there. How I wish I could see what it is like!"

The Way Through the Woods

They shut the road through the woods
     Seventy years ago.
Weather and rain have undone it again,
     And now you would never know
There was once a road through the woods
     Before they planted the trees.
It is underneath the coppice and heath
     And the thin anemones.
Only the keeper sees
     That, where the ring-dove broods,
And the badgers roll at ease,
     There was once a road through the woods.

Yet, if you enter the woods
     Of a summer evening late,
When the night-air cools on the trout-ringed pools
     Where the otter whistles his mate,
(They fear not men in the woods,
     Because they see so few.)
You will hear the beat of a horse's feet,
     And the swish of a skirt in the dew,
Steadily cantering through
     The misty solitudes,
As though they perfectly knew
     The old lost road through the woods ...
But there is no road through the woods.

Rudyard Kipling

Friends

How good to lie a little while

And look up through the tree!

The Sky is like a kind big smile

Bent sweetly over me.

The Sunshine flickers through the lace

Of leaves above my head,

And kisses me upon the face

Like Mother, before bed.

The Wind comes stealing o'er the grass

To whisper pretty things;

And though I cannot see him pass,

I feel his careful wings.

So many gentle Friends are near

Whom one can scarcely see,

A child should never feel a fear,

Wherever he may be.

Abbie Farwell Brown

The Olympic Games

The First Olympic Games

The Olympic Games began in Greece around 3,000 years ago. Historic manuscripts tell us that the first Olympic Games took place in 776 BC in Olympia. These games took place every four years, like today, but back then they were dedicated to the Greek god Zeus. The main sports were running, boxing, wrestling and equestrian events. Only men and boys took part, apart from some female horse-owners in the equestrian events.

After the Romans conquered Greece in 146 BC the games began to decline and were eventually abolished in 393 AD.

The Modern Olympic Games

The Olympic Games were revived by Frenchman Baron Pierre de Coubertin. He was a very keen sportsman and believed that sport could promote peace by bringing nations together. In 1894 he created the International Olympic Committee and the first modern Olympic Games were held in Athens, Greece, two years later. The opening ceremony and some of the events took place in the Panathenaic Stadium which was built in 330 BC and restored for the Athens Olympics. More than 300 athletes from 13 countries

competed in the games. The Olympic Games were cancelled during the First and Second World Wars. Apart from this, these inspirational games continue to be held every four years, with the Winter Olympics held in between.

The Olympic rings

The Olympic rings are a famous symbol of the Olympic Games. The symbol was designed in 1913 by Pierre de Coubertin to embody the spirit of the games. The five interlocking rings represent the five continents and when they were designed the five colours, along with the white background, included the colours of every nation that existed at that time. Alongside the Olympic torch, the rings are probably one of the most easily recognisable symbols of the games. Before each games, the torch is lit in Olympia, Greece, then carried in stages to the host city by runners.

The Paralympics

The Paralympic Games are games for athletes with disabilities. They began in 1948 in Stoke Mandeville, UK, when Sir Ludwig Guttmann organised a sports competition for soldiers whose spines had been damaged during the Second World War. Four years later, they were joined by athletes from Holland, and the games have continued to grow ever since. The first Olympic-style games for people with disabilities was held in Rome in 1960, and the first Paralympic Winter Games in Sweden in 1976.

The London 2012 games was the largest Paralympics ever, with record numbers of competitors and spectators. More than 4000 athletes from 164 countries competed, with a record 2.7 million tickets sold and 69% of the British public watching at least some of the games on TV. The games were so successful they changed the way the British public view people with an impairment.

London 2012

The United Kingdom has hosted the Olympic Games three times. The first time was in 1908. These games were due to be held in Rome, but after Mount Vesuvius erupted in 1906, Italy needed to spend a lot of money rebuilding the devastated area around the volcano, so the games were moved to London. The city hosted the games again in 1948.

In 2012 London hosted the games for the third time. The city had to bid against other cities for the huge honour of holding the games and were eventually awarded the event despite fierce competition from cities including Paris, New York, Madrid and Moscow. A huge Olympic Park was built in East London, covering an area the size of 357 football pitches. Nearly nine million tickets were made available to watch more than ten thousand athletes competing in 26 different sports. Over the course of the games an impressive 14 million meals were served to spectators and athletes.

Moonfleet

It must have been past four o'clock in the afternoon, and I was for returning to tea at my aunt's, when underneath the stone on which I sat I heard a rumbling and crumbling, and on jumping off saw that the crack in the ground had still further widened, just where it came up to the tomb, and that the dry earth had so shrunk and settled that there was a hole in the ground a foot or more across. Now this hole reached under the big stone that formed one side of the tomb, and falling on my hands and knees and looking down it, I perceived that there was under the monument a larger cavity, into which the hole opened. I believe there never was boy yet who saw a hole in the ground, or a cave in a hill, or much more an underground passage, but longed incontinently to be into it and discover whither it led. So it was with me; and seeing that the earth had fallen enough into the hole to open a way under the stone, I slipped myself in feet foremost, dropped down on to a heap of fallen mould, and found that I could stand upright under the monument itself.

Now this was what I had expected, for I thought that there had been below this grave a vault, the roof of which had given way and let the earth fall in. But as soon as my eyes were used to the dimmer light, I saw that it was no such thing, but that the hole into which I had crept was only the mouth of a passage, which sloped gently down in the direction of the church. My heart fell to thumping with eagerness and surprise, for I thought I had made a wonderful discovery, and that this hidden way would certainly lead to great things, perhaps even to Blackbeard's hoard; for ever since Mr. Glennie's tale I had constantly before my eyes a vision of the diamond and the wealth it was to bring me. The passage was two paces broad, as high

as a tall man, and cut through the soil, without bricks or any other lining; and what surprised me most was that it did not seem deserted nor mouldy and cob-webbed, as one would expect such a place to be, but rather a well-used thoroughfare; for I could see the soft clay floor was trodden with the prints of many boots, and marked with a trail as if some heavy thing had been dragged over it.

So I set out down the passage, reaching out my hand before me lest I should run against anything in the dark, and sliding my feet slowly to avoid pitfalls in the floor. But before I had gone half a dozen paces, the darkness grew so black that I was frightened, and so far from going on was glad to turn sharp about, and see the glimmer of light that came in through the hole under the tomb. Then a horror of the darkness seized me, and before I well knew what I was about I found myself wriggling my body up under the tombstone on to the churchyard grass, and was once more in the low evening sunlight and the soft sweet air.

Home I ran to my aunt's, for it was past tea-time, and beside that I knew I must fetch a candle if I were ever to search out the passage; and to search it I had well made up my mind, no matter how much I was scared for this moment. My aunt gave me but a sorry greeting when I came into the kitchen, for I was late and hot. She never said much when displeased, but had a way of saying nothing, which was much worse; and would only reply yes or no, and that after an interval, to anything that was asked of her. So the meal was silent enough, for she had finished before I arrived, and I ate but little myself being too much occupied with the thought of my strange discovery, and finding, beside, the tea lukewarm and the victuals not enticing.

L♥ve your heart!

How you heart works

Your heart is amazing! It works round the clock pumping blood all round your body, and most of the time you will not even be aware it is happening.

Your heart contains four chambers: two upper chambers and two lower chambers. Blood comes into the heart through the upper chambers before being squeezed into the lower chambers and then out of the heart into your body. Four valves make sure the blood keeps flowing in the right direction.

First, the blood travels to your lungs where it collects oxygen from the air you breathe.

Then the blood travels back to your heart where it is given a second push and sent on its way around your body. The blood carries oxygen to all of the muscles, to keep you moving, before travelling back to the heart so the whole process can start again.

Blood moves around the body in blood vessels. The vessels that carry blood away from your heart are called arteries. The ones that carry blood back to your heart are called veins.

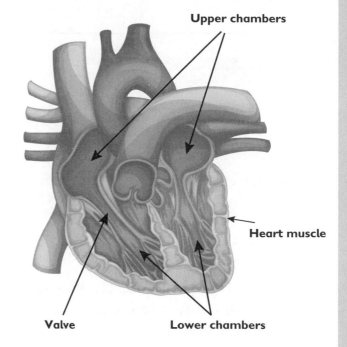

Upper chambers

Heart muscle

Valve

Lower chambers

Finger on the pulse

You can measure how fast your heart is beating by feeling your pulse. Your pulse rate is the number of beats your heart makes each minute. The easiest place to feel it is probably in your wrist, using two fingers from your other hand, like in the picture.

Your heart beats all the time but your pulse rate will change depending on what you are doing. Most people's hearts beat around 80 times a minute

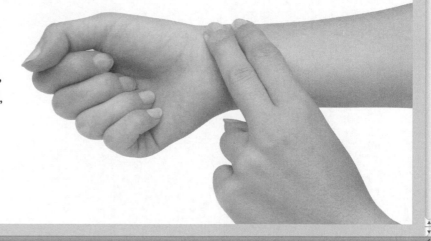

11

when they are sitting down, but while you are exercising your heart will beat faster because your muscles need more oxygen. Your lungs will also work harder too, making you breathe faster to breathe in more oxygen.

Try taking your pulse when you are sitting down. Then run around for a while and take it again. What was the difference?

_____

Heart facts

Did you know, your heart:

* beats around 100,000 times every day

* pumps blood through a staggering 60,000 miles of blood vessels in your body

* is about the same size as your fist.

_____

Heart healthy

You can help to keep your hardworking heart healthy by leading a healthy lifestyle. That includes eating a varied and balanced diet that includes at least five portions of fruit and vegetables every day. There are easy ways to add more fruit and veg to your diet. Try adding a chopped banana to your breakfast cereal, or take some raw carrot stick to school to eat at break time.

It is also important to get plenty of exercise every day. Making your heart and lungs work harder helps to keep them strong. You do not need to visit a gym or sports centre to stay fit either. Kick a ball around in your garden, dance to your favourite music with your friends, or go on a bike ride with your family. Anything that gets your heart beating faster will do you good, and if you are having fun too, that is even better!

4 Who or what *broods* in the poem?

_____

1 mark

5 Explain **two** things that the words *misty solitudes* suggest about the wood.

_____

_____

_____

2 marks

Questions 6–7 are about *Love your heart!*

6 Match each statement to the correct body part.

Blood enters this part of the heart.	lower chambers
Blood leaves through this part of the heart.	veins
Blood travels away from the heart in these vessels.	upper chambers
Blood travels towards the heart in these vessels.	arteries

1 mark

7 Where is the easiest place to feel your pulse?

_____

1 mark

Total marks .... /10   How am I doing?

27

Inference in Fiction 1

> ## These questions are about *The Secret Garden.*

1 What evidence is there in the first paragraph to suggest that *The Secret Garden* is set in the past?

_____

_____ 1 mark

2 How does the first paragraph suggest that Mary's health is not very good at the start of the extract?

_____

_____ 1 mark

3 What does the second paragraph suggest is responsible for the improvement in Mary's appetite?

_____

_____ 1 mark

4 In the paragraph beginning *"It's th' air of th' moor…* Martha compares Mary with the people in her family.

How do these comparisons help the reader to understand what life is like for Martha's family? Identify one similarity and one difference.

_____

_____

_____

_____ 2 marks

28

5 Look at the paragraph beginning *At first each day...* (page 3).

Explain how the descriptions of the wind in this paragraph suggest that it had both a positive and a negative impact on Mary.

Use evidence from the text to support your answer.

_____

_____

_____

_____

_____

_____

_____

_____

_____

3 marks

6 How can you tell that Martha is a servant in the household?

_____

_____

1 mark

29

7 What evidence is there in the text to suggest what Ben Weatherstaff's job is?

_____

_____ 1 mark

8 *spread out on all sides and climb up to the sky*

How do these words make the reader feel about the moor?

_____

_____ 1 mark

9 *"I like you! I like you!" she cried out.*

Explain how Mary's reaction to the robin in this part of the text supports the idea that she is lonely.

Use evidence from the text to support your answer.

_____

_____

_____

_____

_____ 2 marks

Total marks .... /13   How am I doing?

These questions are about *Moonfleet*.

1 What evidence is there in the text that suggests that the boy does not live with his parents?

_____

_____

_____

1 mark

2 The tunnel is described as *a wonderful discovery*....

Look at the paragraph that begins *Now this was what I had expected*... (page 9).

Explain how the description of the passage in this paragraph supports the idea that the boy is not the first person to discover it.

Use evidence from the text to support your answer.

_____

_____

_____

_____

_____

2 marks

Inference in Fiction 2

1 In the paragraph beginning *Now this was what I had expected,* what evidence is there that the boy believes Mr Glennie's tale about Blackbeard's hoard?

_____

_____

_____

_____ 1 mark

2 In the paragraph beginning *So I set out down the passage,* the boy is glad to be back in the *soft sweet air* of the churchyard.

What does this suggest about the air in the passage?

_____

_____

_____

_____ 1 mark

3 How can you tell that the boy's aunt is angry at the end of the extract?

_____

_____

_____

_____ 1 mark

Total marks .... /6   How am I doing?

These questions are about *The Olympic Games*.

1   Why was the first modern Olympic Games held in Greece?

_____

_____

_____

1 mark

2   How do the Olympic rings *embody the spirit of the games*?

Give **two** ways.

1. _____

_____

2. _____

_____

2 marks

3   How did the 2012 Paralympic games change the British public's view of people with an impairment?

_____

_____

_____

_____

1 mark

4 Look at the final paragraph.

Why was competition to host the 2012 Olympics *fierce*?

_____

_____

_____

1 mark

5 Using information from *The Olympic Games*, tick a box for each statement to say whether it is a **fact** or an **opinion**.

	Fact	Opinion
It is impressive that 14 million meals were served during the 2012 Olympic Games.		
It is a huge honour to host the Olympic Games.		
Baron Pierre de Coubertin revived the Olympic Games.		
The Olympic Park covered an area the size of 357 football pitches.		

1 mark

Total marks .... /6   How am I doing?

34

> These questions are about *Love Your Heart!*

1 Why is your heart *amazing*?

_____

_____

1 mark

2 How does the information on page 12 make it sound easy to lead a healthy lifestyle?

Give **two** ways.

1. _____

2. _____

2 marks

3 Using information from *Love Your Heart!*, tick a box for each statement to say whether it is a **fact** or an **opinion**.

	Fact	Opinion
The easiest place to feel your pulse is probably in your wrist.		
Blood carries oxygen to your muscles.		
If exercise is fun too, that is even better.		
While you are exercising, your heart will beat faster.		

1 mark

Total marks ..../4   How am I doing?

Inference in Poetry

> **Questions 1–2 are about *The Way Through the Woods.***

1   Why does only the keeper see that there used to be a road through the woods?

_____

_____

_____

1 mark

2   In the second verse the poet says that in the late evening, *You will hear the beat of a horse's feet...* (page 5).

Explain how the description of the woods in the rest of the poem supports the idea that there cannot really be people travelling through the wood.

Use evidence from the text to support your answer.

_____

_____

_____

_____

_____

_____

_____

_____

2 marks

Questions 3–4 are about *Friends*.

3 *kisses me upon the face*

How do these words make the reader feel about the Sun?

_____

_____

1 mark

4 *A child should never feel a fear,*
Wherever he may be.

Explain how these lines support the idea that you can take comfort from being in the natural world.

Use evidence from the text to support your answer.

_____

_____

_____

_____

_____

_____

_____

_____

2 marks

Total marks .... /6   How am I doing?

Predicting Events

1 **a)** Based on what you have read, what do you think Mary will do next?

Use evidence from the text to support your prediction.

_____

_____

_____

_____

_____

_____
2 marks

b) Based on what you have read, do you think Mary will find a way into the garden?

Use evidence from the text to support your prediction.

_____

_____

_____

_____
2 marks

Question 2 is about _Moonfleet._

2 Based on what you have read, what does the last paragraph suggest might happen to the boy next?

Use evidence from the paragraph to support your prediction.

_____

_____

_____

_____

_____

_____

_____

_____

2 marks

Total marks .... /6   How am I doing?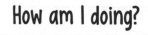

Whole Text Meaning

Question 1 is about *The Secret Garden.*

1 **a)** In the first half of the extract, there is evidence that spending time outside is improving Mary's health.

Find and **copy** the sentence on page 4 that shows that this is still happening at the end of the extract.

_____

_____
1 mark

b) How does her health improve? Give **two** ways.

1. _____

2. _____
2 marks

Question 2 is about *The Olympic Games.*

2 **a)** The text contains information about the number of athletes who took part in the first modern games in 1896 and the 2012 games in London.

How does this information help you to understand how the Olympic Games have developed?

_____

_____
1 mark

b) Give two pieces of information that are given about the London 2012 games but are not given about the 1896 games.

1. _____

2. _____
2 marks

Question 3 is about *Moonfleet.*

3 **a)** How does the boy's mood change once he is under the ground? Compare how he felt at first to how he felt later.

_____

_____ 1 mark

b) **Find** and **copy** two groups of words that show how his mood changes from his initial feeling of excitement.

1. _____

2. _____ 2 marks

Question 4 is about *Love Your Heart!*

4 **a)** The first sentence of the text tells you, *Your heart is amazing!*

Which section of the text gives the most compelling information to support this?

_____ 1 mark

b) The final section says *You can help to keep your hardworking heart healthy...*

Find and **copy** a group of words from each of these sections that tells you how hard your heart works.

How your heart works _____

Finger on the pulse _____ 2 marks

Total marks .... /12   How am I doing? 😊 😐 😣

Question 1 is about *Friends*.

1 Why does the poet compare the Sunshine with Mother?

_____

_____

_____

_____ 1 mark

Question 2 is about *The Way Through the Woods*.

2 Look at these lines.

They fear not men in the woods,

Because they see so few.

Apart from these lines, how does the poem show that very few people go into the woods? Use evidence from the text to support your answer.

_____

_____

_____

_____ 2 marks

Question 3 is about *The Secret Garden*.

3 How does Mary work out that the tree that the robin lives in is inside the walled garden?

_____

_____ 1 mark

Questions 4–5 are about *The Olympic Games.*

4 Tick a box for each statement to say whether it is a **fact** or an **opinion.**

	Fact	Opinion
The Olympic rings are probably one of the most easily recognisable symbols of the games.		
The Paralympics began in 1948.		
The ancient Romans did not like the Olympics.		
Mount Vesuvius erupted in 1906.		

1 mark

5 *devastated area* (page 8)

What does this tell you about the eruption of Vesuvius in 1906?

_____

_____

1 mark

Question 6 is about *Love Your Heart!*

6 Why is it *staggering* that we have 60,000 miles of blood vessels in our bodies?

_____

_____

1 mark

Total marks .... /7   How am I doing?

Answers

The KS2 English Reading test assesses eight elements of the national curriculum (see table below). These references are included within the answers to show which element each question is assessing to help you to track children's progress.

Content domain reference

2a give / explain the meaning of words in context
2b retrieve and record information / identify key details from fiction and non-fiction
2c summarise main ideas from more than one paragraph
2d make inferences from the text / explain and justify inferences with evidence from the text
2e predict what might happen from details stated and implied
2f identify / explain how information / narrative content is related and contributes to meaning as a whole
2g identify / explain how meaning is enhanced through choice of words and phrases
2h make comparisons within the text

Question	Requirement	Marks	Content domain ref.
\multicolumn{4}{c}{**Page 4-5 Choosing the Meaning of Words in Context**}			
1	interesting	1	2a
2	stared	1	2a
3	moving	1	2a
4	sauntered	1	2a
\multicolumn{4}{c}{**Page 6-7 Giving the Meaning of Words in Context**}			
1	roared	1	2a
2	bare	1	2a
3	scarlet, redbreast	2	2a
4	darting	1	2a
5	scornfully	1	2a
6	rude	1	2a
7	forgotten	1	2a
8	pale	1	2a
\multicolumn{4}{c}{**Page 8-9 Explaining the Meaning of Words in Context**}			
1	The weather and rain have destroyed the road.	1	2a
2	The badgers feel relaxed in the woods.	1	2a
3	The horse's feet sound like a drum beating.	1	2a
4	The sky is friendly. The sky is happy.	2	2a
5	The sunlight shining through the gaps in the leaves makes them looks like lace.	1	2a
6	The sunlight feels gentle on the poet's face.	1	2a
\multicolumn{4}{c}{**Page 10-11 Finding Meaning from Words**}			
1	The information was written a long time ago.	1	2g
2	Baron Pierre de Coubertin brought back the Olympic Games.	1	2g
3	London had to fight hard to be awarded the games.	1	2g
4	The narrator's emotions were so strong they made his heart beat faster.	1	2g

5	There is very little room in the opening of the passage so the boy has to wriggle to get his body through it.	1	2g
6	Hole, cavity, cave, passage	4	2g

Page 12-13 Progress Test 1			
1	observed	1	2a
2	store	1	2a
3	widened	1	2a
4	The narrator thinks about the story all the time.	1	2g
5	abandoned	1	2a
6	Many people have walked along the passage.	1	2g

Page 14-15 Finding Information in Fiction 1			
1	Any two from: waking in her tapestried room; eating her breakfast in the nursery; gazing out of the window; going outside.	2	2b
2	porridge	1	2b
3	Award 1 mark for answers where the child has circled her eyes.	1	2b
4	12	1	2b
5	a) fireplace, b) deliberately, c) clipped, d) chirp	4	2b

Page 16-17 Finding Information in Fiction 2			
1	After four o'clock in the afternoon.	1	2b
2	Mr Glennie	1	2b
3	a) two paces, b) as high as a tall man	2	2b
4	the soil	1	2b
5	Something heavy has been dragged over the floor.	1	2b
6	a) edge, b) feet-first, c) earth, d) darkness	4	2b

Page 18-19 Finding Information in Poetry			
1	70 years	1	2b
2	Any two from: ring-dove broods; badgers roll at ease; otter whistles its mate.	2	2b
3	whistle	1	2b
4	trout	1	2b
5	a tree	1	2b
6	the Sky; the Wind	2	2b
7	Award 1 mark for answers where the child has circled the tree's leaves.	1	2b
8	Mother	1	2b

Page 20-21 Finding Information in Non-Fiction 1			
1	When did the first Olympic Games take place? — 776 BC To which god were they dedicated? — Zeus How often did the games take place? — Every 4 years	Award 2 marks for all three correct; award 1 mark for two correct.	2b

45

2	Any two from: running, boxing, wrestling, equestrian events.	2	2b
3	Promote peace by bringing nations together.	1	2b
4	357	1	2b
5	The ancient Olympics were abolished → 393 AD The Panathenaic Stadium was built → 1913 The Olympic symbol was designed → 1976 The first Paralympic Winter Games were held → 330 BC	Award 1 mark if all correct.	2b
6	Because Mount Vesuvius erupted and Italy needed to spend lots of money on rebuilding the area around the volcano, so they could not afford to host the games.	1	2b

Page 22-23 Finding Information in Non-Fiction 2

1	valves	1	2b
2	<table><tr><td></td><td>True</td><td>False</td></tr><tr><td>Human hearts have two chambers.</td><td></td><td>✓</td></tr><tr><td>Arteries carry blood away from the heart.</td><td>✓</td><td></td></tr><tr><td>Your pulse rate is how many times your heart beats in a minute.</td><td>✓</td><td></td></tr><tr><td>Your heart is around the same size as your head.</td><td></td><td>✓</td></tr></table>	Award 1 mark if all correct.	2b
3	It increases.	1	2b
4	oxygen	1	2b
5	100,000 times a day	1	2b
6	fruit, vegetables	2	2b
7	They get stronger.	1	2b

Page 24-25 Summarising Main Ideas

1	Nature reclaims land when humans abandon it.	1	2c
2	You should never feel lonely when you are surrounded by nature.	1	2c
3	<table><tr><td></td><td>True</td><td>False</td></tr><tr><td>Mary spends time in the garden because there is nothing to do indoors.</td><td>✓</td><td></td></tr><tr><td>Mary does not like Ben Weatherstaff.</td><td></td><td>✓</td></tr><tr><td>Martha thinks that being outside is good for Mary's health.</td><td>✓</td><td></td></tr><tr><td>Mary is not curious about the walled garden.</td><td></td><td>✓</td></tr></table>	Award 1 mark if all correct.	2c
4	<table><tr><td></td><td>True</td><td>False</td></tr><tr><td>The events in the extract take place in a churchyard.</td><td>✓</td><td></td></tr><tr><td>The boy is not interested in what is under the grave.</td><td></td><td>✓</td></tr><tr><td>The passage is man-made.</td><td>✓</td><td></td></tr><tr><td>The boy is the first person to have walked along the passage.</td><td></td><td>✓</td></tr></table>	Award 1 mark if all correct.	2c

	Page 26-27 Progress Test 2		
1	Because he was on his way home for tea.	1	2b
2	He reaches out his hands in front of him; he slides his feet slowly	2	2b
3	Any two from: coppice, heath, anemones.	2	2b
4	ring-doves	1	2b
5	Misty suggests you can't see clearly in the woods. Solitude suggests you will be alone if you go to the woods.	2	2a
6	Blood enters this part of the heart. → upper chambers Blood leaves through this part of the heart. → lower chambers Blood travels away from the heart in these vessels. → arteries Blood travels towards the heart in these vessels. → veins	Award 1 mark if all correct.	2b
7	Your wrist	1	2b
	Page 28-30 Inference in Fiction 1		
1	Award 1 mark for one of the following acceptable points: 1. The room is heated with a fire in a hearth. 2. The children play with sticks and stones.	1	2d
2	Award 1 mark for one of the following acceptable points: 1. She is described as having *slow blood*. 2. She has a *thin body*. 3. She has *dull eyes*.	1	2d
3	Being outside all day makes Mary hungry.	1	2d
4	Martha says that like Mary, the people in her family are hungry but unlike her, they do not always have enough to eat, suggesting that they do not have very much money.	2	2d
5	The wind rushes at her and makes it difficult for her to move, but it is also improving her health because she has to fight against it. Examples of evidence of the wind having a negative impact include: 'she hated the wind which rushed at her face' or it 'roared and held her back as if it were some giant she could not see'. Examples of evidence of the wind having a positive impact include: 'the big breaths of rough fresh air blown over the heather filled her lungs with something which was good for her whole thin body' or that it 'whipped some red colour into her cheeks and brightened her dull eyes'.	3	2d
6	The fact that she wakes up before Mary every morning to make the fire in Mary's room.	1	2d
7	He works outside with a spade.	1	2d
8	The moor is so big it is all you can see apart from the sky.	1	2d

9	Award 1 mark for a response that identifies an acceptable point but does not give evidence. Award 2 marks for a response that identifies at least one acceptable point **and** gives a piece of evidence. • Mary tries to communicate with the robin, and believes that she can, because the text says 'she were sure that he would understand and answer her'. This suggests she has no human company. • Mary imagines that the robin wants her to play with it, because she thinks it is saying '"Let us both chirp and hop and twitter. Come on! Come on!"'	2	2d
	Page 31-32 Inference in Fiction 2		
1	In the final paragraph, the narrator talks about going 'home' to his aunt's, suggesting that he lives with her.	1	2d
2	Award 1 mark for a response that identifies an acceptable point but does not give evidence. Award 2 marks for a response that identifies at least one acceptable point **and** gives a piece of evidence. • The tunnel is clean inside, because the text says it is not 'mouldy and cob-webbed'. • The tunnel has obviously been used by a lot of people because the floor is 'trodden with the prints of many boots'. • There is a mark on the floor caused by someone dragging 'some heavy thing' over it.	2	2d
3	Award 1 mark for one of the following: • The boy is sure the tunnel will lead to something exciting because the text says the passage will 'certainly lead to great things, perhaps even to Blackbeard's hoard'. • The boy thinks about the wealth Blackbeard's treasure 'was to bring' him, suggesting he is certain the treasure is there and he will find it.	1	2d
4	The fact that the boy notices how pleasant the air in the churchyard is suggests that the air in the passage does not smell sweet and may smell unpleasant.	1	2d
5	The narrator explains that the aunt says very little when she is angry. He also says that his meal was silent, suggesting that the aunt is not speaking because she is angry.	1	2d
	Page 33-34 Inference in Non-Fiction 1		
1	It seemed an appropriate place to hold the first modern games because that is where the ancient games were held.	1	2d
2	1. The five rings represent the five continents. 2. The colours of the rings included the colours of the flags of every nation that existed when the symbol was designed in 1913.	Award 1 mark for each acceptable point given	2d
3	As more people had access to viewing the games they were able to see that disability did not mean they could not compete.	1	2d
4	Because it is a 'huge honour' to host the games, so lots of cities tried very hard to win the bid.	1	2d

	Fact	Opinion
It is impressive that 14 million meals were served during the 2012 Olympic Games.		✓
It is a huge honour to host the Olympic Games.		✓
Baron Pierre de Coubertin revived the Olympic Games.	✓	
The Olympic Park covered an area the size of 357 football pitches.	✓	

Award 1 mark if all correct. — 2d

Page 35 Inference in Non-Fiction 2

1 Because it beats all the time throughout your whole life. — 1 — 2d

2 Award 1 mark for reference to any of these acceptable points, up to 2 marks.
1. Easy to eat more fruit and vegetables, e.g.
   - adding a chopped banana to your breakfast cereal
   - taking raw carrot sticks to school.
2. Easy access to exercise opportunities, e.g.
   - kicking a ball around in your garden
   - dancing to your favourite music with friends
   - going on a bike ride with family.

— 2 — 2d

3

	Fact	Opinion
The easiest place to feel your pulse is probably in your wrist.		✓
Blood carries oxygen to your muscles.	✓	
If exercise is fun too, that is even better.		✓
While you are exercising, your heart will beat faster.	✓	

Award 1 mark if all correct. — 2d

Page 36-37 Inference in Poetry

1 Only the keeper knows the woods well enough to know that there was once a road there; very few other people go there. — 1 — 2d

2

Acceptable points	Likely evidence (accept paraphrase)
People could not really be travelling through the wood because the road has been closed for a long time and has disappeared.	*They shut the road through the woods seventy years ago.* *There was once a road through the woods.* *Weather and rain have undone it again.* *It is underneath coppice and heath.* *There is no road through the woods.*

2 — 2d

	Award 1 mark for an acceptable point without evidence from the poem. Also award 1 mark for a relevant quotation taken from the poem without a link to an acceptable point.		
3	The Sun is gentle/friendly/kind.	1	2d
4	Because the natural world is always around us, wherever we are, we do not need to worry about feeling lonely. We know this because in the previous line, natural things are described as being 'gentle friends'.	2	2d

Page 38-39 Predicting Events

1 a)	**Acceptable points (can be implied)** / **Evidence** 1. Follow the robin. — Mary likes the robin / Mary is bored and lonely / Mary knows that the robin lives in the garden 2. Ask Ben Weatherstaff about the garden. — Mary has spoken to him before / The robin is referred to as 'Ben Weatherstaff's robin' so he may know something about it 3. Look for a door into the garden. — Mary wishes she could see inside the garden	2	2e
1 b)	**Acceptable points (can be implied)** / **Evidence** Yes — The title of the book is *The Secret Garden,* suggesting some of the story will take place in the garden Mary really wants to see the garden Mary wishes she could see inside the garden For 1a) and 1b) award 2 marks for an acceptable prediction supported by evidence from the text. Award 1 mark for either an acceptable point or a relevant piece of evidence from the text.	2	2e
2	**Acceptable points (can be implied)** / **Evidence** The boy takes a candle and goes back to explore the passage. — Text says the boy realises he needs a candle if he is going to explore the tunnel Text says the boy has made up his mind he would explore the passage	2	2e

Page 40-41 Whole Text Meaning

1 a)	*Poor little thin, sallow, ugly Mary—she actually looked almost pretty for a moment*	1	2f
1 b)	Any two of: her appetite improves/she gets colour in her cheeks/her eyes brighten/she looks pretty for a moment.	2	2h
2 a)	The scale of the increase in the number of athletes taking part in the Olympic Games shows how much bigger the games have become.	1	2h
2 b)	Any two of: the size of the Olympic Park/the number of meals served/ the number of sports/the number of tickets sold.	2	2f

3 a)	The boy goes from being eager and surprised to being afraid.	1	2f
3 b)	1. *the darkness grew so black that I was frightened* 2. *a horror of the darkness seized me*	2	2f
4 a)	Heart facts	1	2f
4 b)	Likely answers include: How your heart works: *It works round the clock pumping blood all round your body* Finger on the pulse: *Your heart beats all the time*	2	2h

Page 42-43 Progress Test 3

1	Because most people think that mothers are kind and gentle, and the Sunshine is kind and gentle when it kisses the child's face.	1	2d
2		2	2d

Acceptable points — **Likely evidence (accept paraphrase)**

Acceptable points	Likely evidence (accept paraphrase)
1. The road is closed.	*shut seventy years ago* *there is no road through the woods* *it is underneath coppice and heath*
2. Animals feel safe.	*ring-dove broods* *badgers roll at ease* *otter whistles his mate*
3. Only the keeper goes there.	*only the keeper sees* *misty solitudes*

Award 2 marks for an acceptable point supported with evidence from the text. Award 1 mark for an acceptable point or a relevant piece of evidence from the text.

3	By comparing the position of the tree from both sides of the orchard.	1	2d
4		1	2d

	Fact	Opinion
The Olympic rings are probably one of the most easily recognisable symbols of the games.		✓
The Paralympics began in 1948.	✓	
The ancient Romans did not like the Olympics.		✓
Mount Vesuvius erupted in 1906.	✓	

5	The eruption caused a lot of serious damage.	1	2g
6	It is very surprising that so many miles of blood vessels would fit into the human body.	1	2d

Progress Test Chart

Progress Test 1

Q	Topic	✓ or ✗	See Page
1	Choosing the Meaning of Words in Context		4
2	Choosing the Meaning of Words in Context		4
3	Giving the Meaning of Words in Context		6
4	Explaining the Meaning of Words in Context		8
5	Giving the Meaning of Words in Context		6
6	Explaining the Meaning of Words in Context		8

Progress Test 2

Q	Topic	✓ or ✗	See Page
1	Finding Information in Fiction		14
2	Finding Information in Fiction		14
3	Finding Information in Poetry		18
4	Finding Information in Poetry		18
5	Explaining the Meaning of Words in Context		8
6	Finding Information in Non-Fiction		20
7	Finding Information in Non-Fiction		20

Progress Test 3

Q	Topic	✓ or ✗	See Page
1	Inference in Poetry		36
2	Inference in Poetry		36
3	Inference in Fiction		28
4	Inference in Non-Fiction		33
5	Explaining the Meaning of Words in Context		8
6	Inference in Non-Fiction		33

What am I doing well in?

_____

_____

What do I need to improve?

_____

_____